ACKNOWLEDGEMENTS

Publishing Director	Piers Pickard
Publisher	Tim Cook
Commissioning Editor	Jen Feroze
Illustrators	Andy Mansfield Sebastien Iwohn
Designer	Andy Mansfield
Print production	Larissa Frost, Nigel Longuet

Published in March 2017 by Lonely Planet Global Ltd
CRN: 554153
ISBN: 978 1 78657 527 2
www.lonelyplanetkids.com

Printed in China

10 9 8 7 6 5 4 3 2 1

Lonely Planet Offices

AUSTRALIA
The Malt Store, Level 3, 551 Swanston St,
Carlton, Victoria 3053
T: 03 8379 8000

IRELAND
Unit E, Digital Court, The Digital Hub,
Rainsford St, Dublin 8

USA
124 Linden St, Oakland, CA 94607
T: 510 250 6400

UK
240 Blackfriars Rd, London SE1 8NW
T: 020 3771 5100

STAY IN TOUCH lonelyplanet.com/contact

MIX
Paper from responsible sources
FSC www.fsc.org FSC™ C021741

Paper in this book is certified against the Forest Stewardship Council™ standards. FSC™ promotes environmentally responsible, socially beneficial and economically viable management of the world's forests.

lonely planet kids

first words FRENCH

Illustrated by
Andy Mansfield & Sebastien Iwohn

hello

---

bonjour

(bon-jhoor)

bonjour

ice cream

glace

(glas)

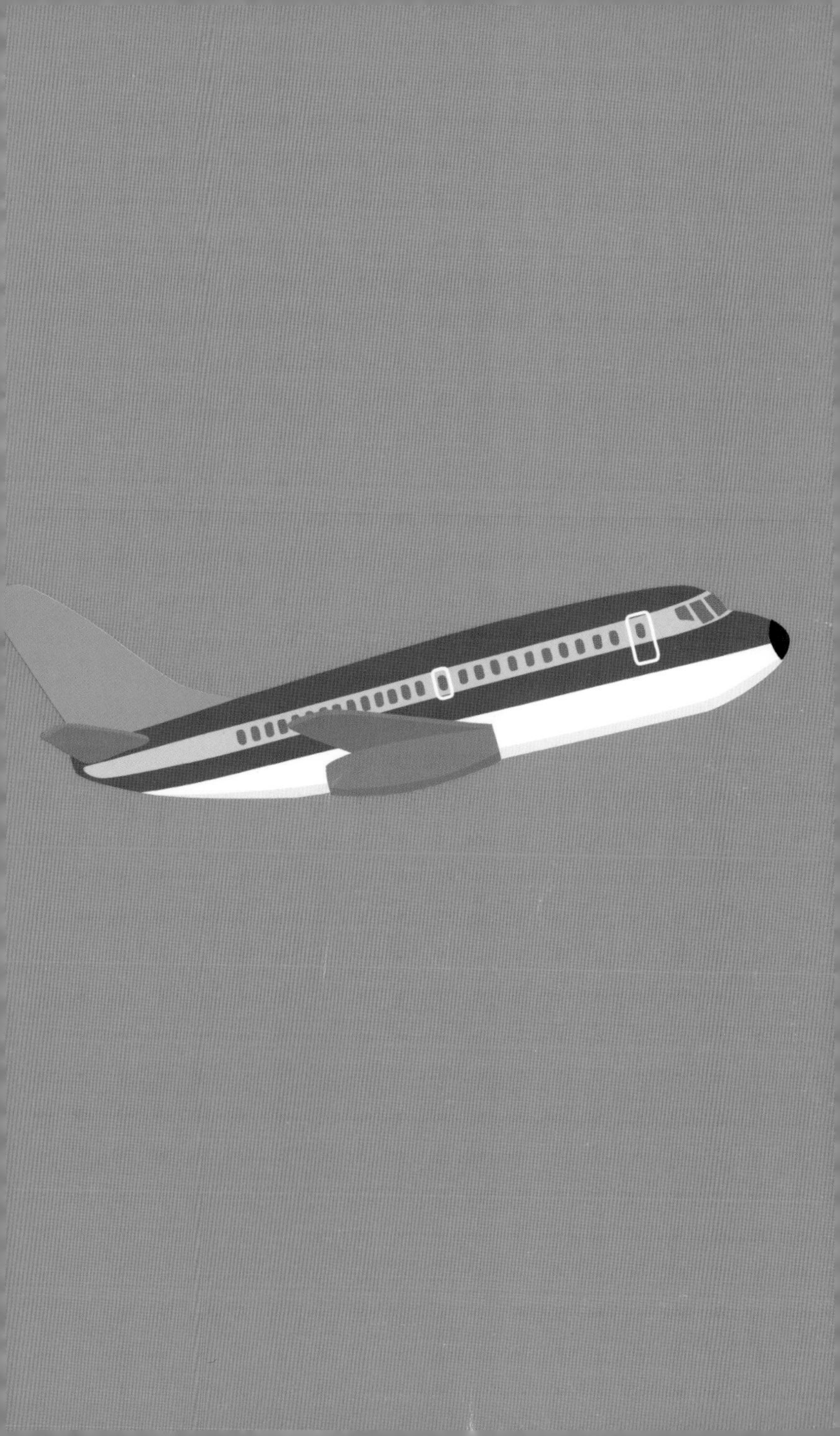

horse

---

cheval

(shuh-val)

french fries

frites

(freet)

swimming pool

piscine

(pee-seen)

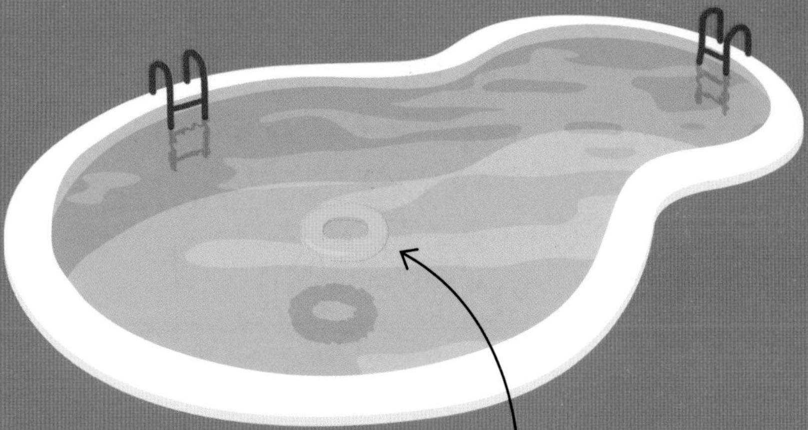
rubber ring
bouée
(boo-eh)

cheese

---

fromage

(fro-mah-jh)

towel

---

serviette

(sair-vee-et)

doctor

---

docteur

(dok-ter)

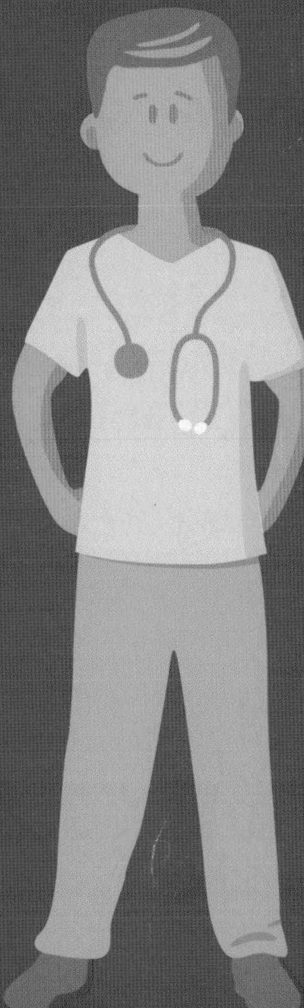

apple

pomme

(pom)

worm

ver

(vair)

beach

---

plage

(plah-jh)

bicycle

---

vélo

(vay-loh)

airport

---

aéroport

(air-roh-por)

juice

---

jus

(jhoo)

bakery

boulangerie

(boo-lon-jher-ee)

boulangerie

shoes

chaussures

(shoh-sewr)

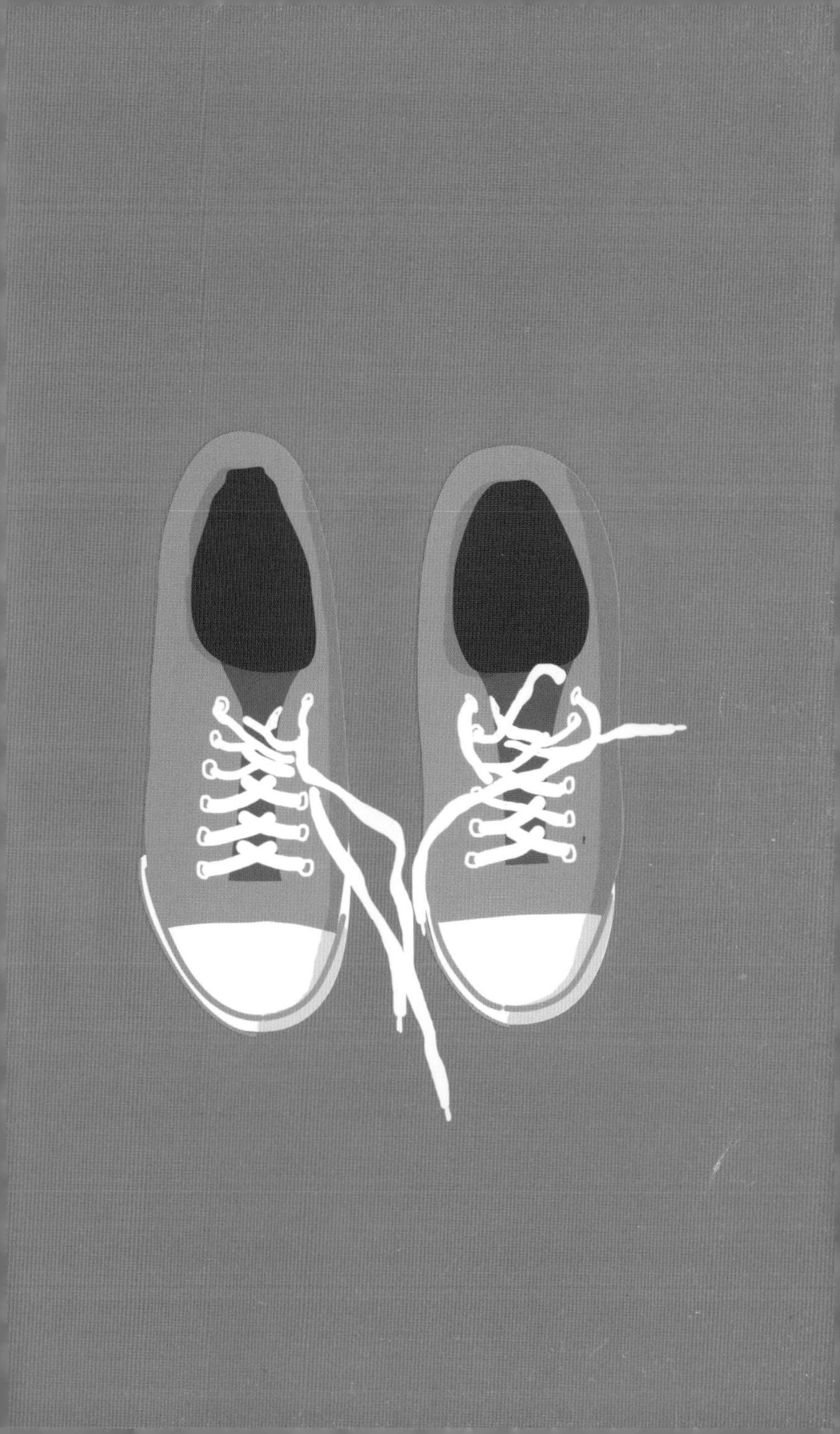

phone

---

téléphone

(teh-leh-fon)

post office

bureau de poste

(bew-roh duh po-st)

restaurant

---

restaurant

(res-toh-ron)

hotel

---

hôtel

(oh-tel)

hôtel

milk

lait

(lay)

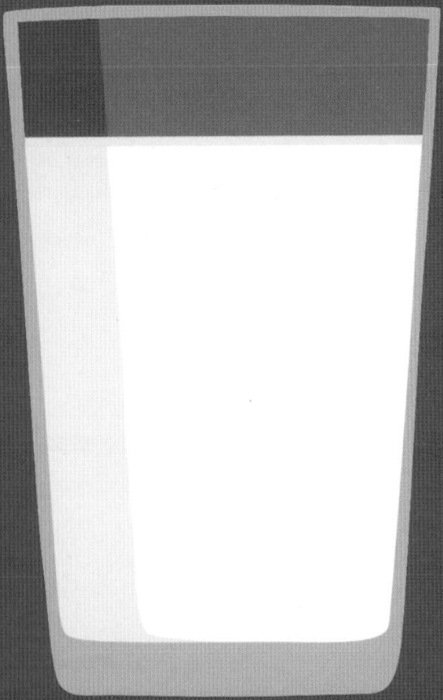

chocolate

---

chocolat

(sho-koh-la)

car

---

voiture

(vwa-tewr)

hat

---

chapeau

(sha-poh)

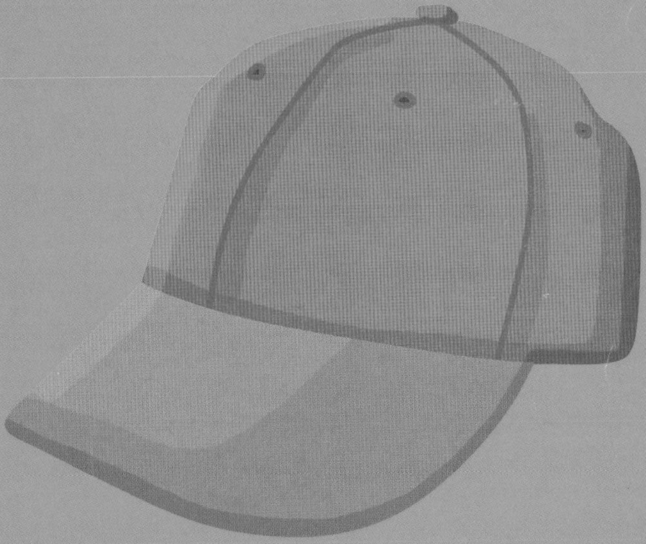

sunglasses

lunettes de soleil

(loo-net duh so-lay)

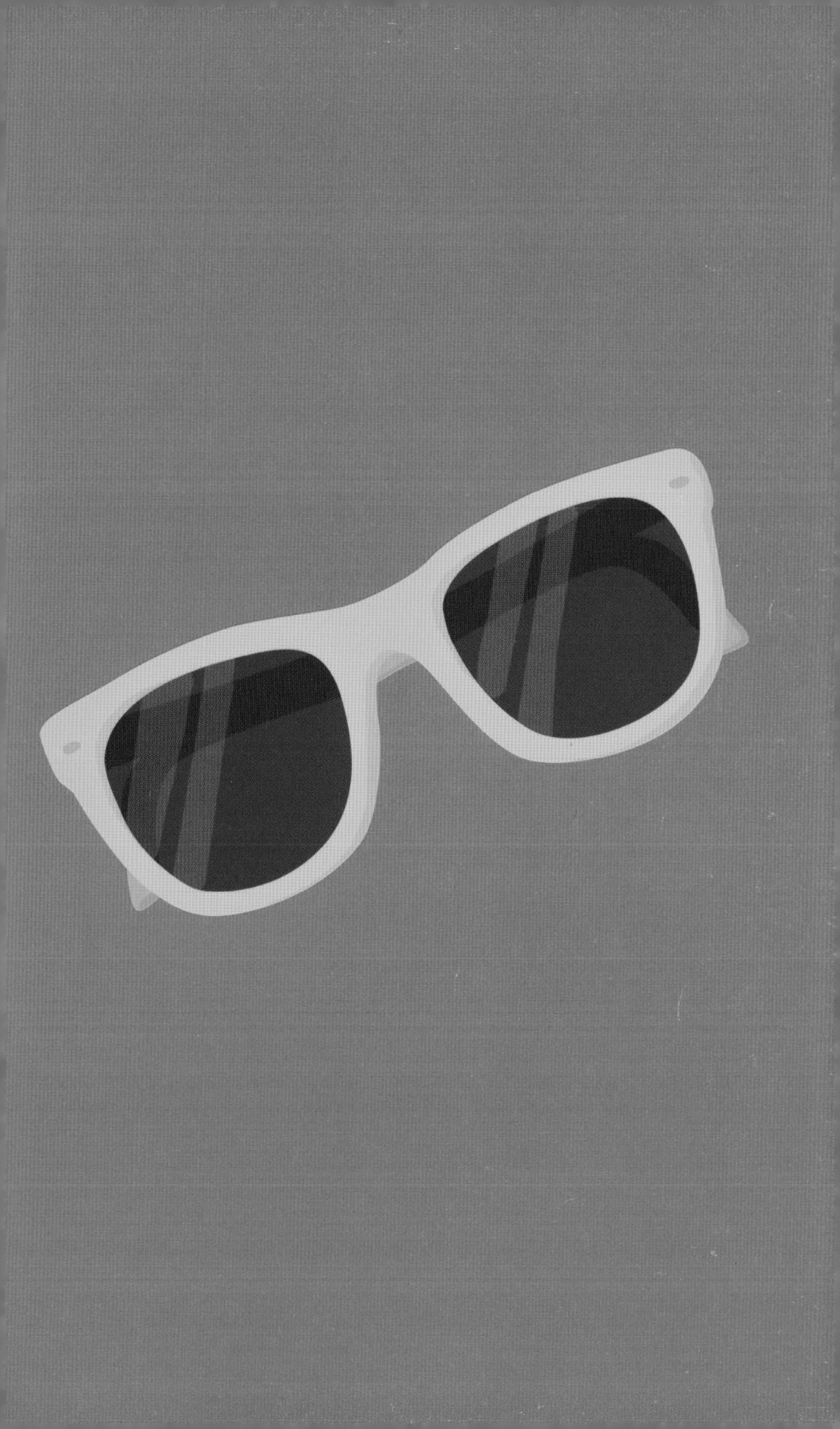

chicken

poulet

(poo-lay)

train / train

(tra)

station

---

gare

(gar)

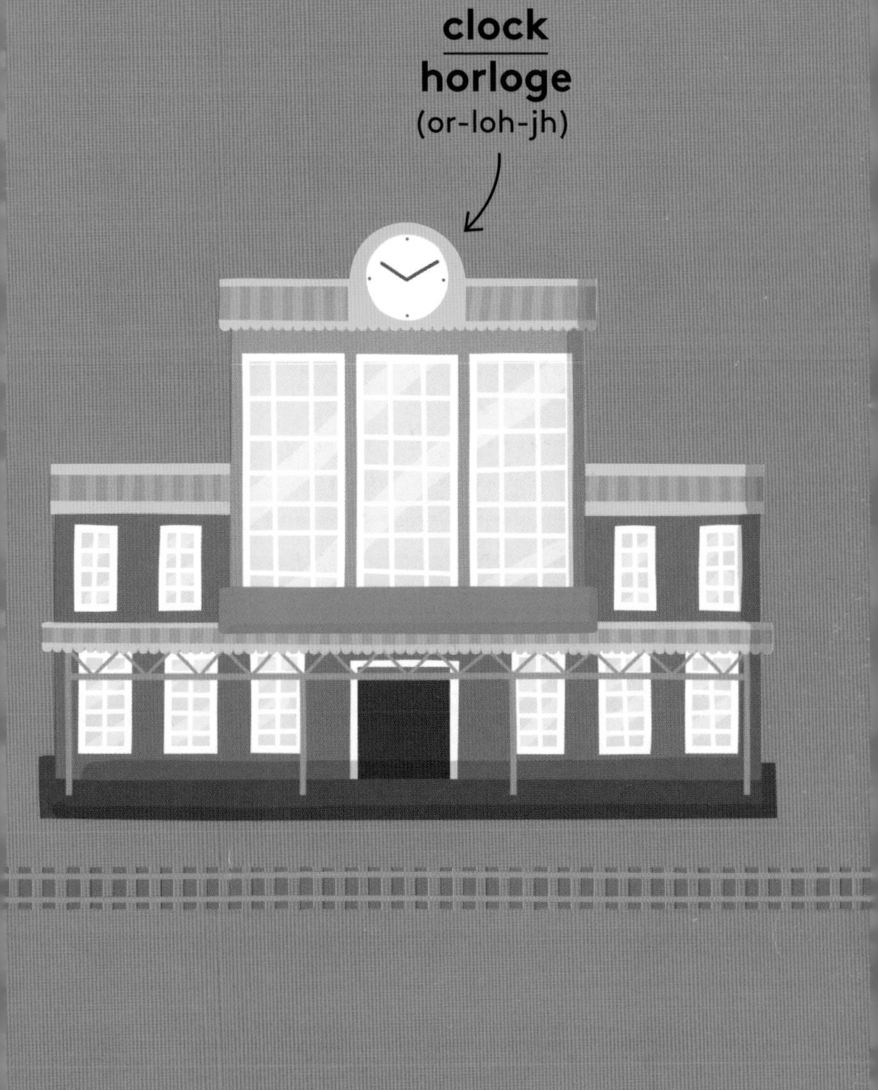
clock
horloge
(or-loh-jh)

toilet

---

toilettes

(twa-let)

bed

lit

(lee)

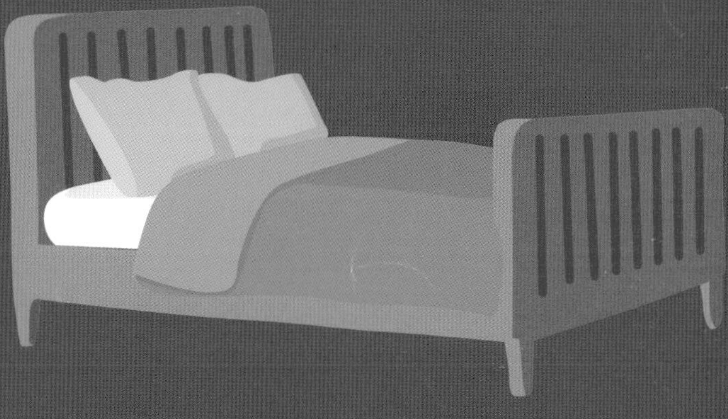

house

---

maison

(may-zon)

chimney

cheminée

(shuh-mi-nay)

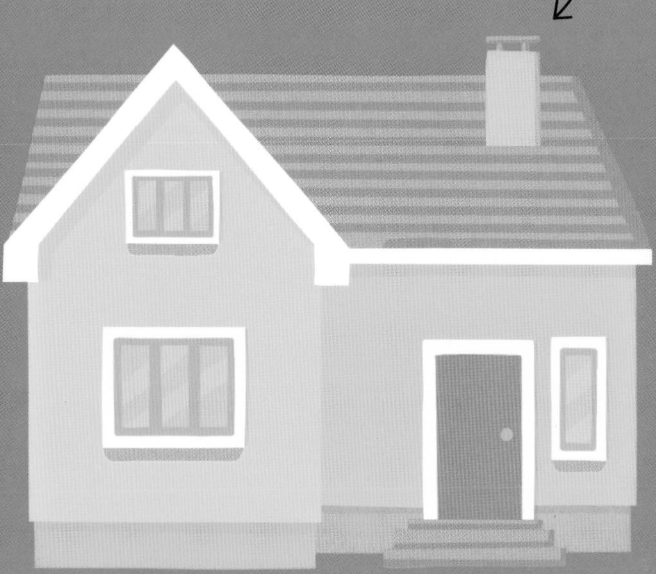

trousers

---

pantalon

(pon-ta-lon)

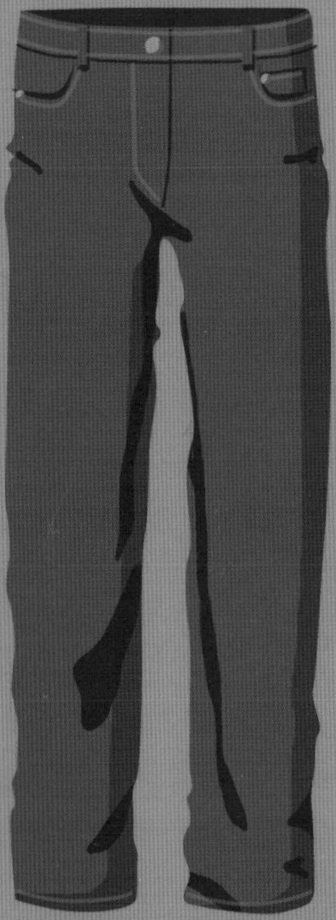

suitcase

valise

(va-leez)

plate

---

assiette

(ass-ee-et)

knife

---

couteau

(koo-toh)

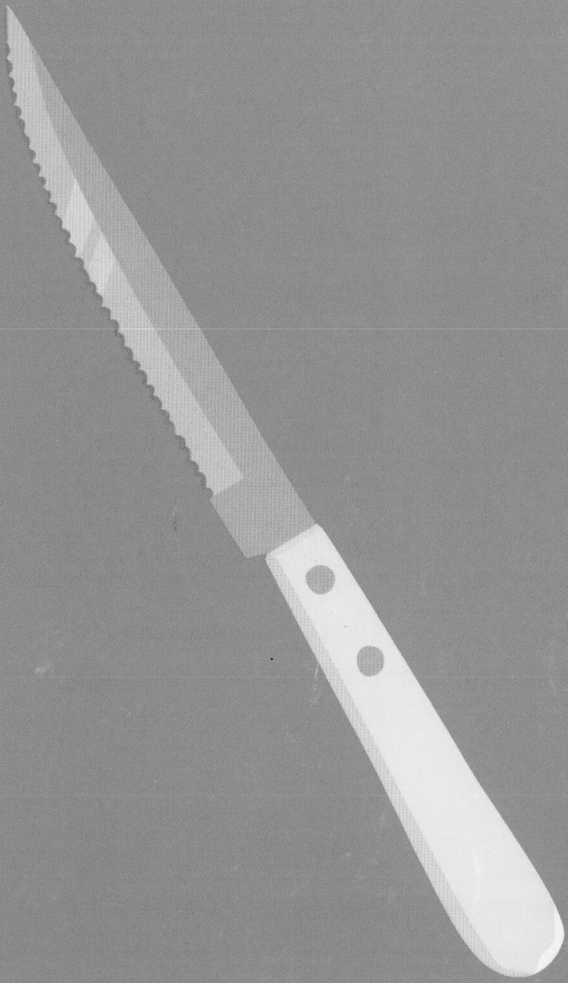

fork

fourchette

(for-shet)

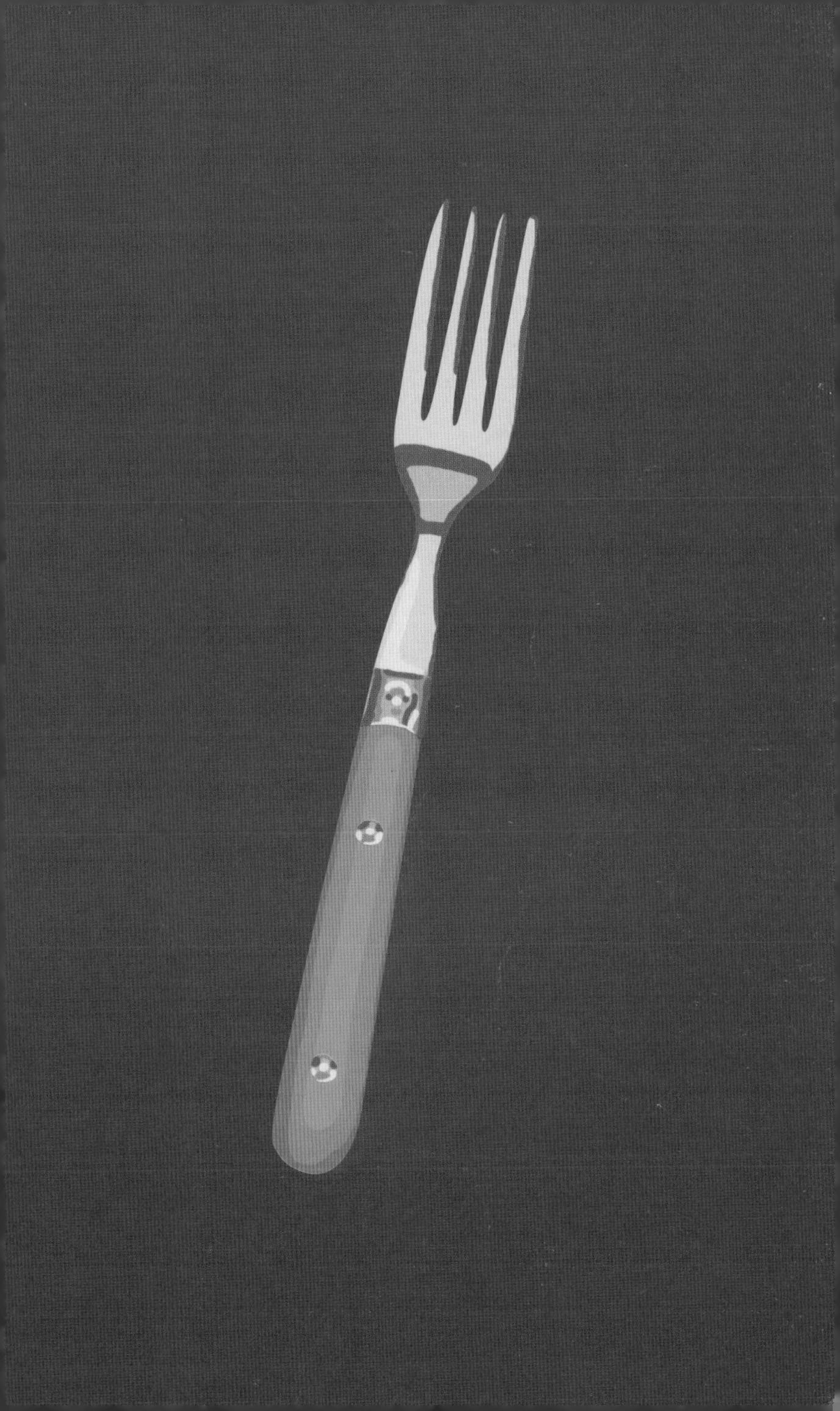

spoon

---

cuillère

(kwee-air)

computer

---

ordinateur

(or-dee-na-ter)

mouse

souris

(soo-ree)

book

---

livre

(leev-ruh)

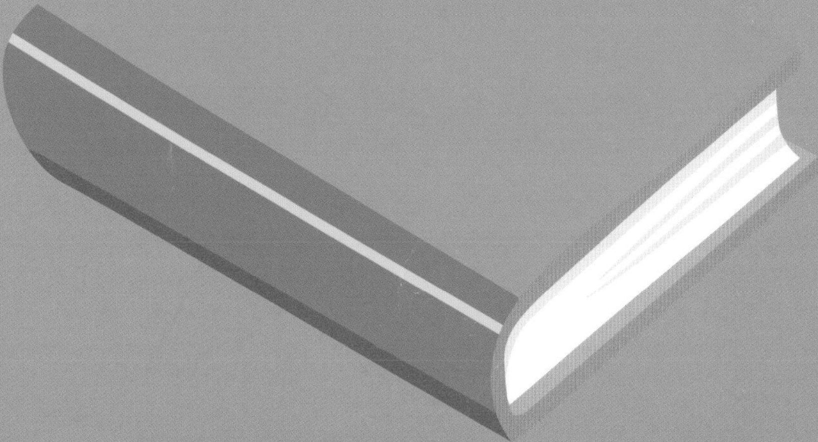

sandwich

---

sandwich

(sond-weech)

yes

oui

(wee)

no

non

(n-on)

cinema

---

cinéma

(see-nay-ma)

cinéma

park

---

parc

(park)

menu

---

carte

(kart)

La Carte

passport

---

passeport

(pass-por)

PASSEPORT

police officer

policier

(po-lee-syay)

key

---

clé

(klay)

ticket

---

billet

(bee-yay)

ADMIT
ONE

pineapple

---

ananas

(a-na-nas)

rain

pluie

(plwee)

snow

---

neige

(neh-jh)

sun

---

soleil

(so-lay)

tree

---

arbre

(ah-bruh)

flower

---

fleur

(fl-uhr)

cake

gâteau

(ga-toh)

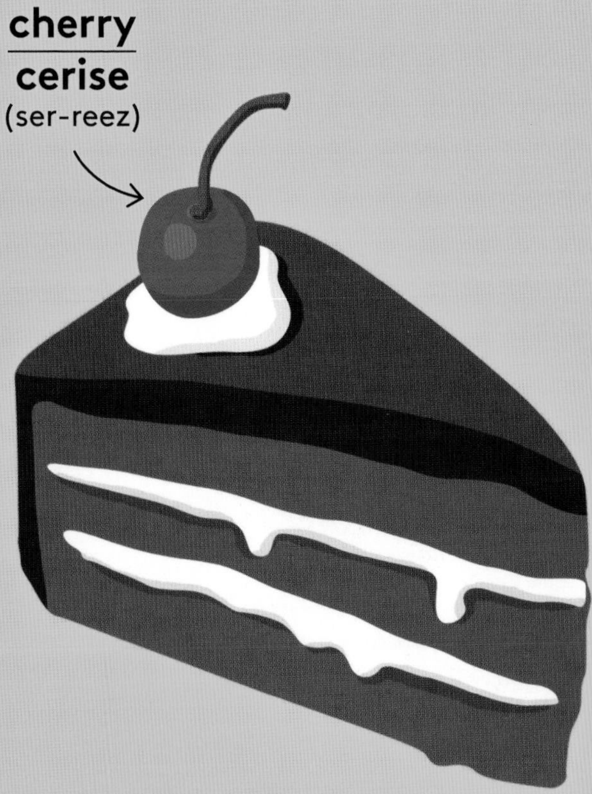
cherry
cerise
(ser-reez)

ball

---

ballon

(ba-lon)

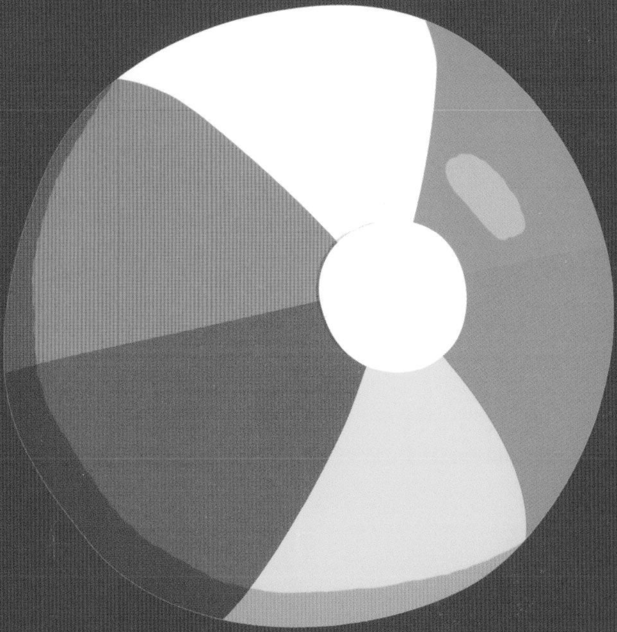

bird

---

oiseau

(wa-zoh)

egg

œuf

(erf)

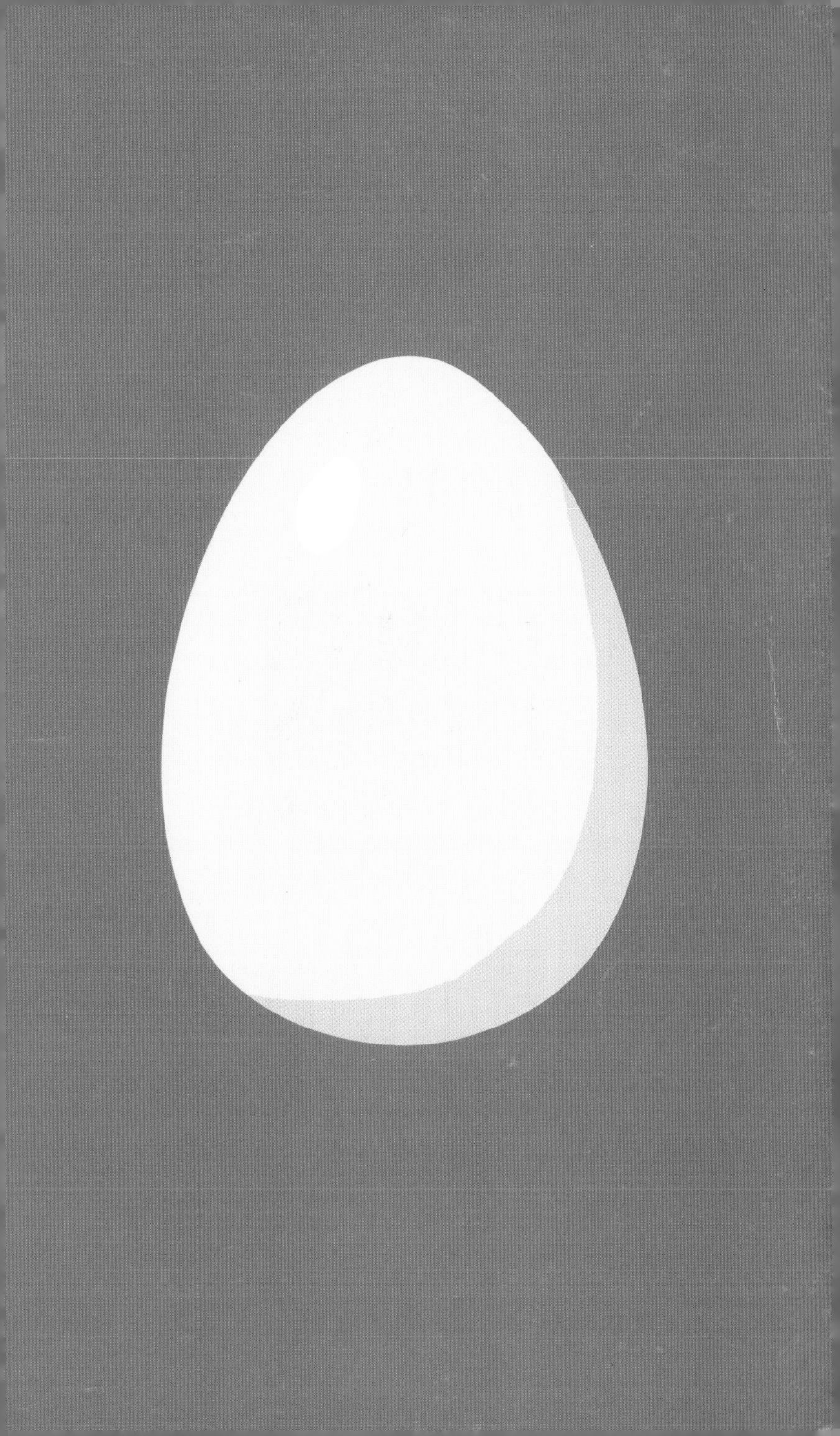

umbrella

---

parapluie

(pa-ra-plwee)

rabbit

---

lapin

(la-pa)

money

---

argent

(ar-jhon)

bank

---

banque

(bong-k)

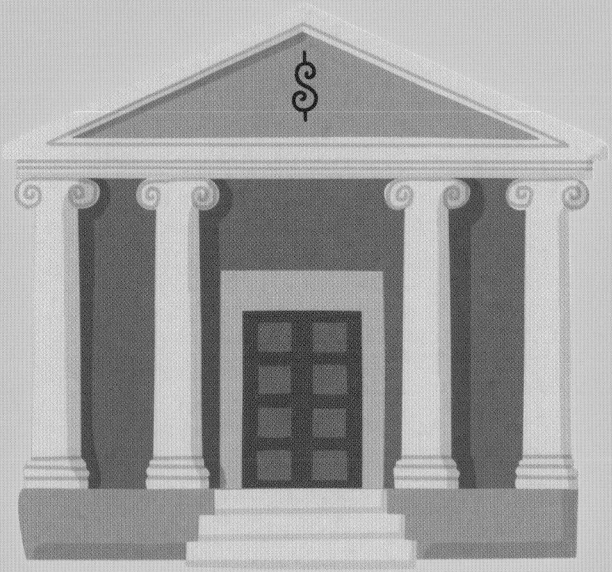

mouse

---

souris

(soo-ree)

scarf

écharpe

(eh-sharp)

gloves

gants

(gon)

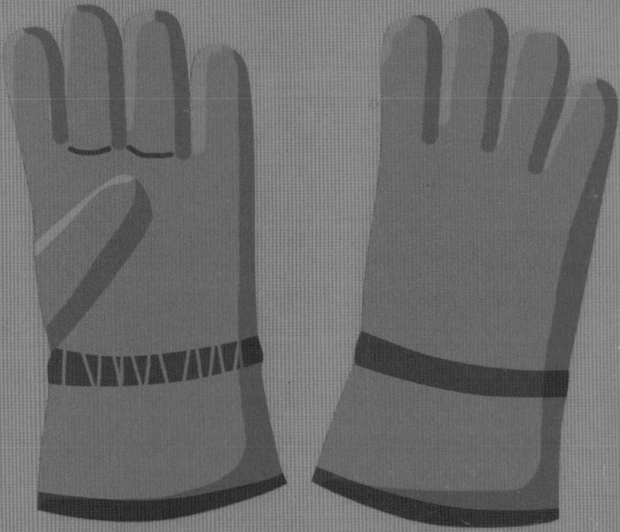

coat

---

manteau

(mon-toh)

hospital

hôpital

(o-pee-tal)

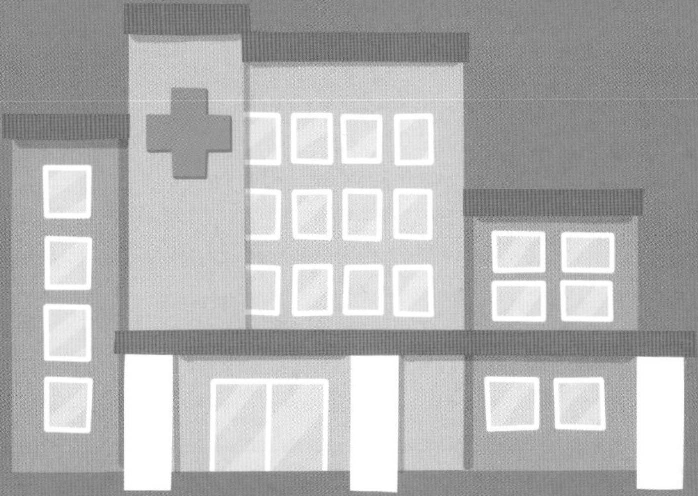

chair

---

chaise

(shez)

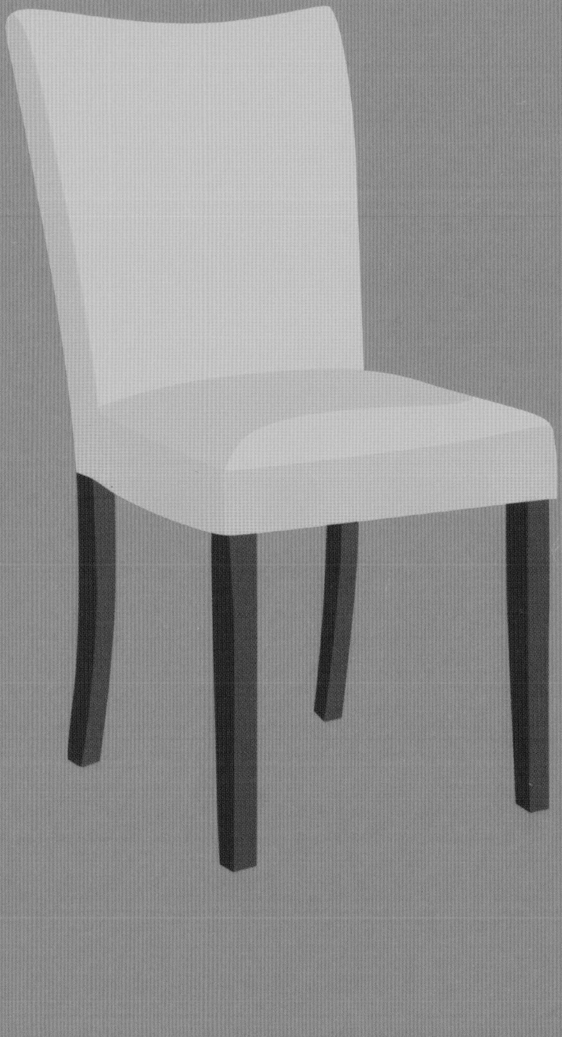

table

---

table

(ta-bluh)

toothbrush

---

brosse à dents

(bross a don)

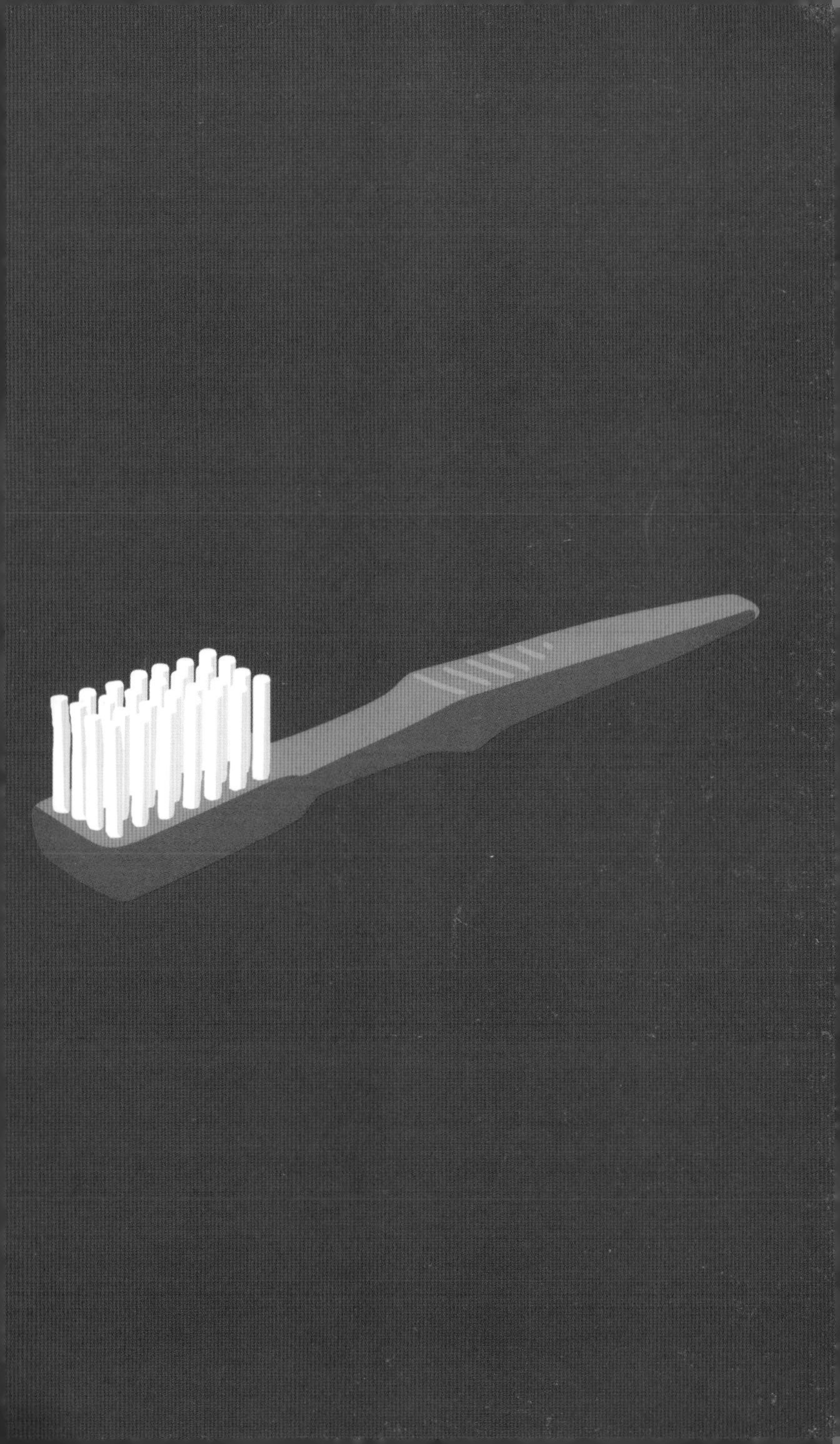

toothpaste

dentifrice

(don-tee-frees)

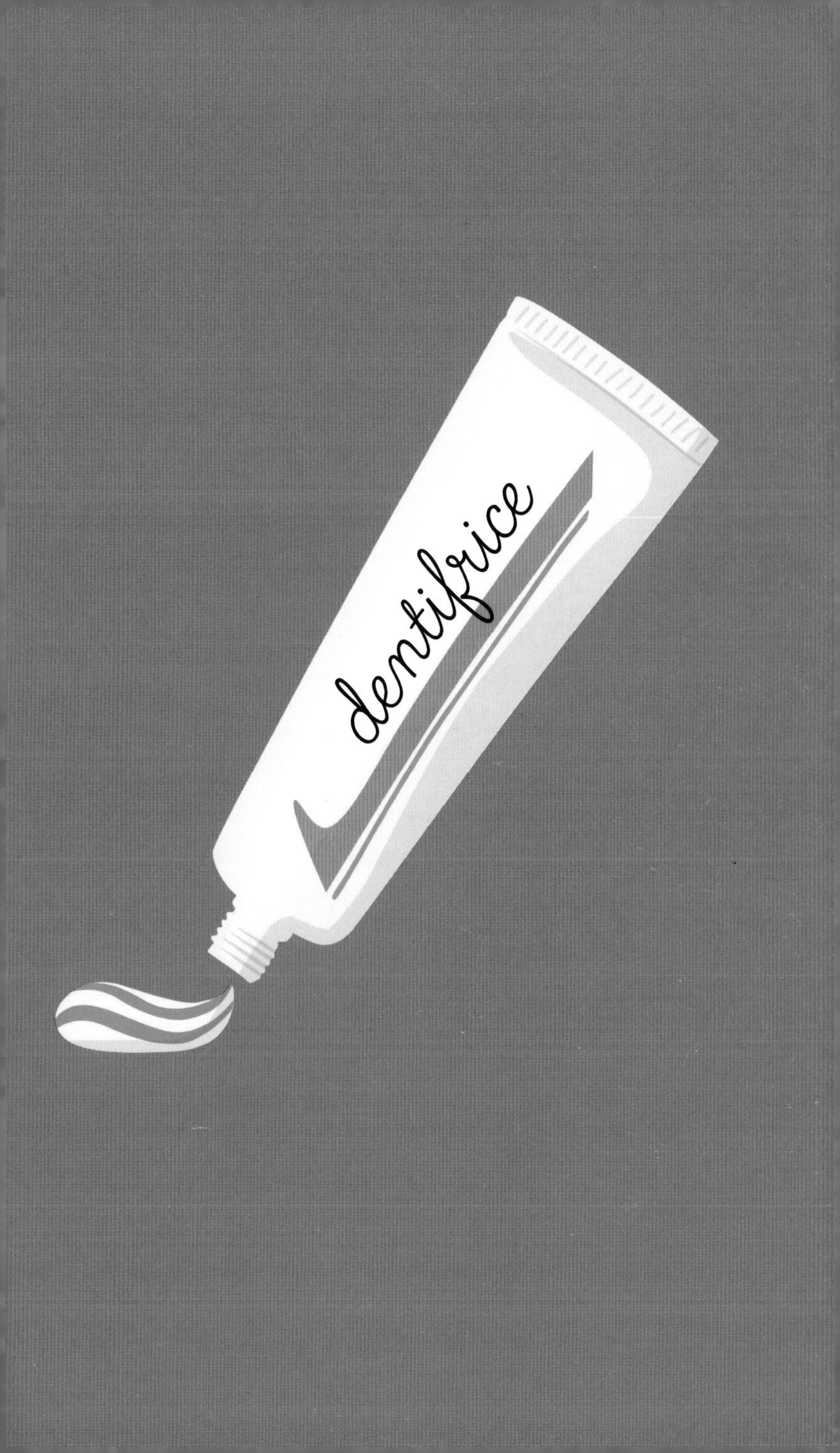
dentifrice

sun cream

crème solaire

(krem so-lair)

spf 50

lion

---

lion

(lee-on)

elephant

éléphant

(eh-leh-fon)

monkey

singe

(san-jh)

water

---

eau

(oh)

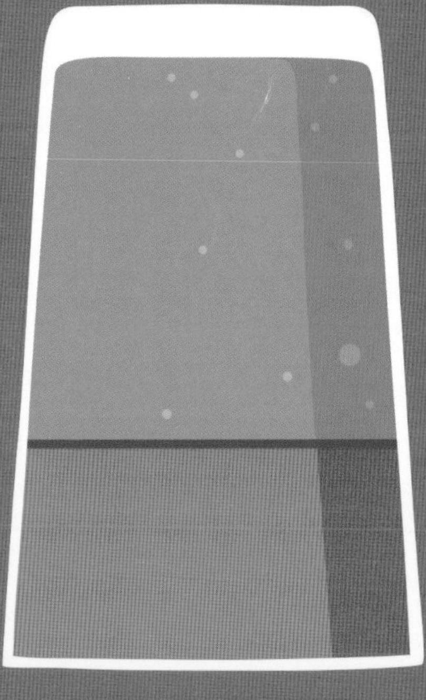

supermarket

supermarché

(soo-pair-mar-shay)

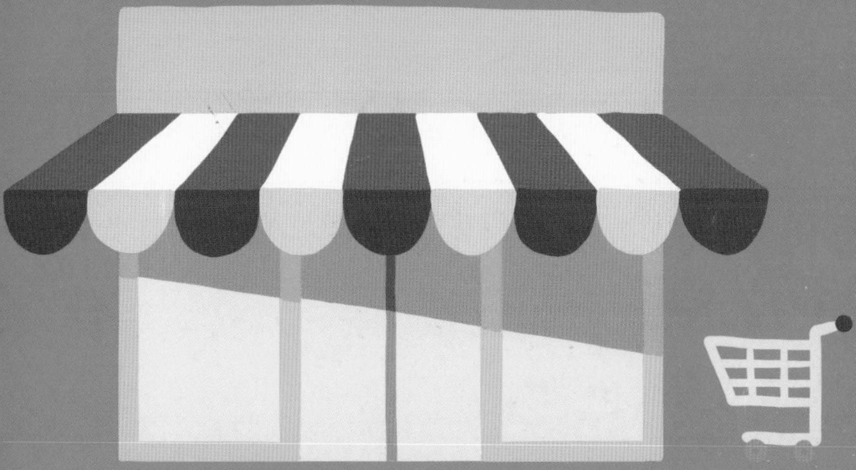

trolley
chariot
(sha-ree-oh)

cat

---

chat

(sha)

bus

autobus

(o-toh-boos)

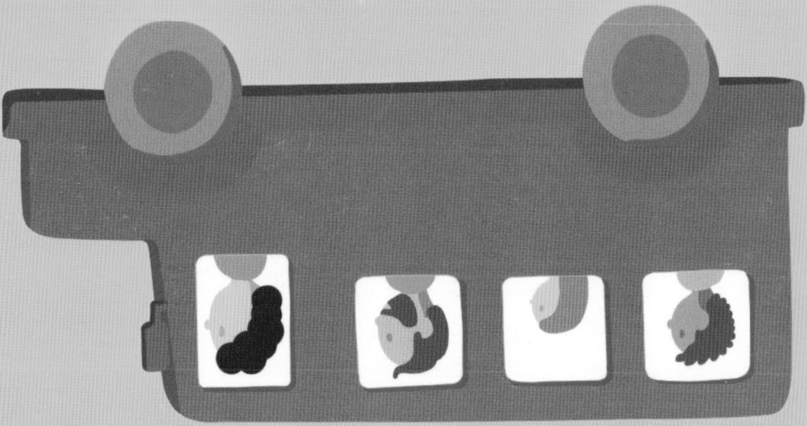

dress

---

robe

(rob)

dog

---

chien

(shee-uh)

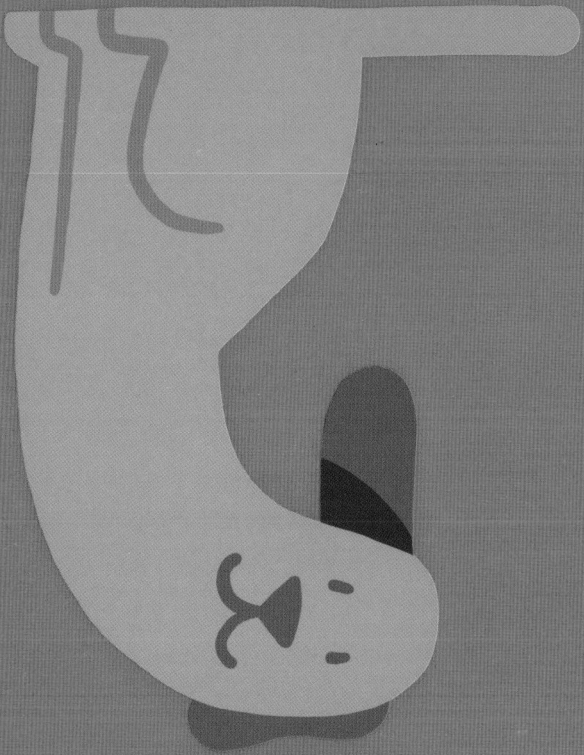

banana

---

banane

(ba-nan)

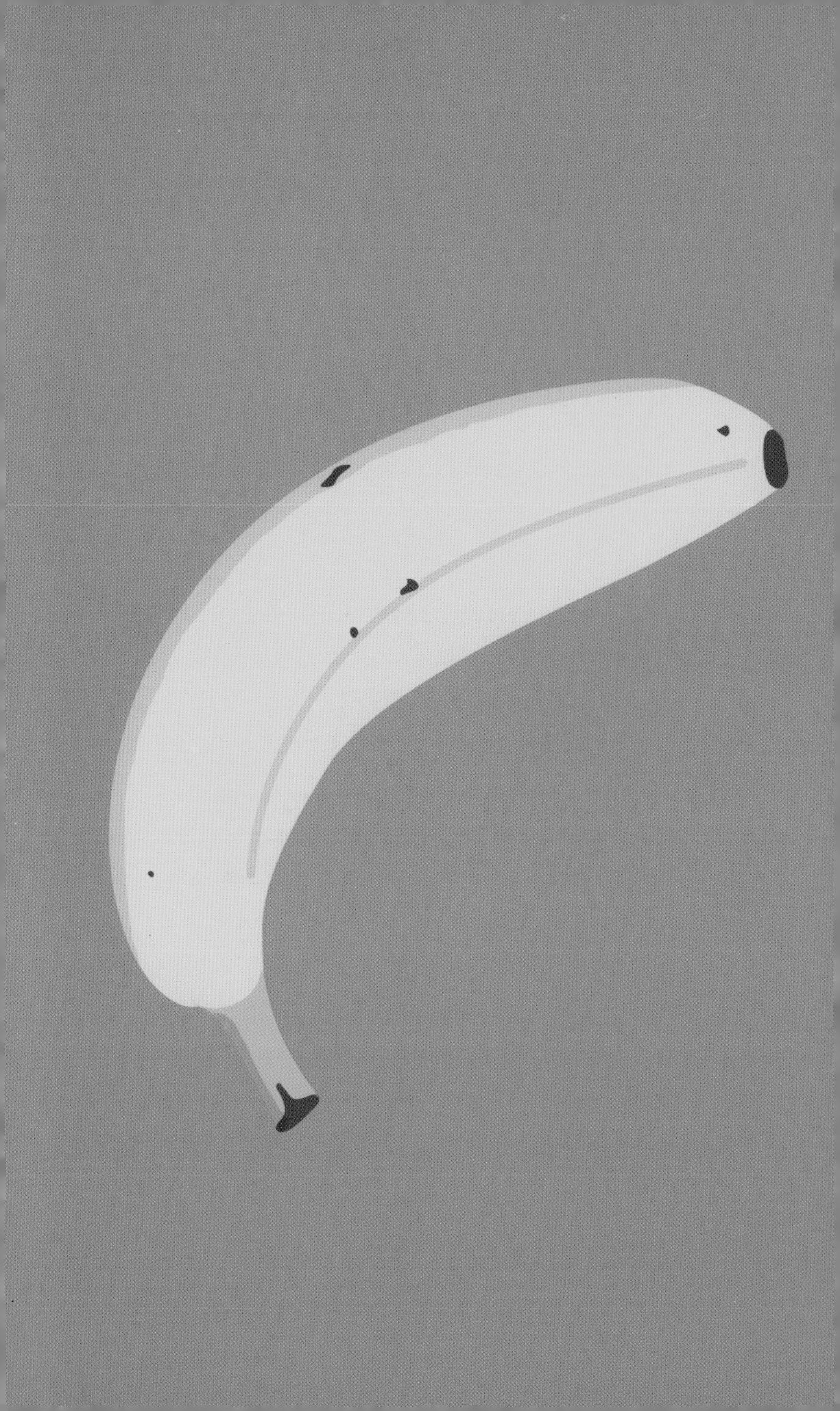

carrot

carotte

(ka-rot)

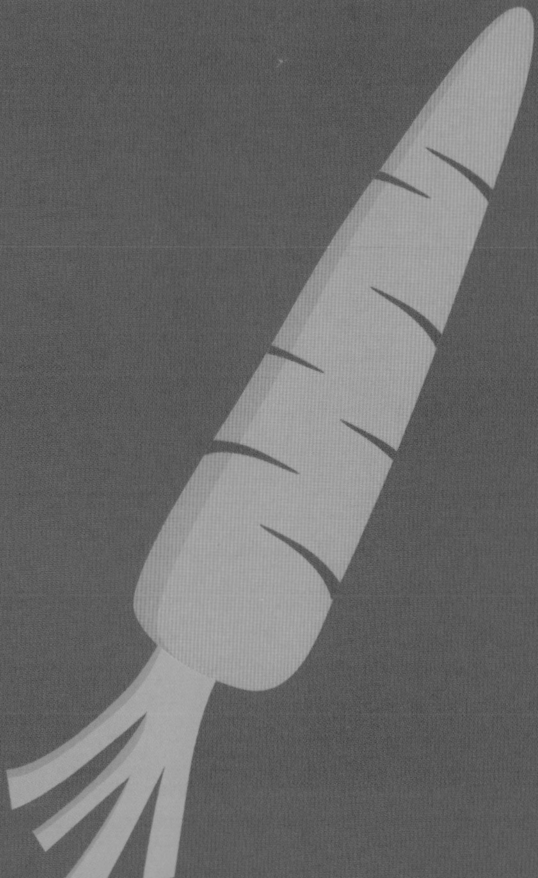

taxi

---

taxi

(tak-see)

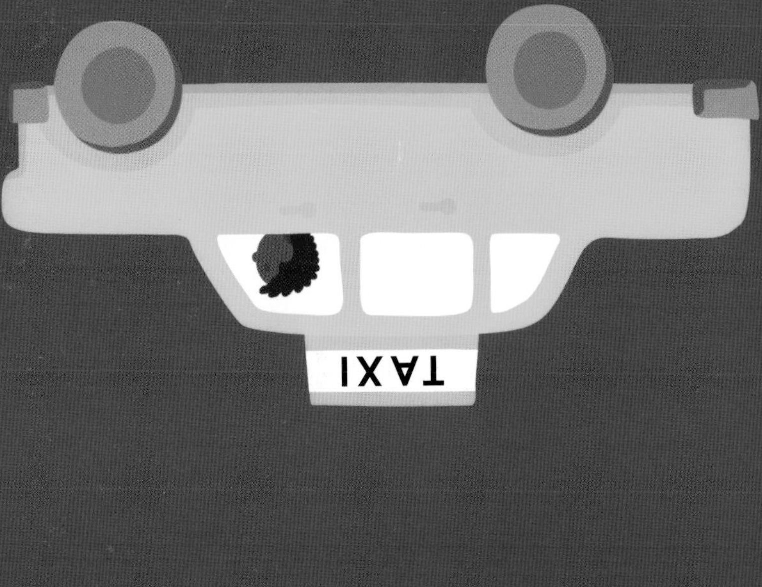
TAXI

t-shirt

t-shirt

(tee-shert)

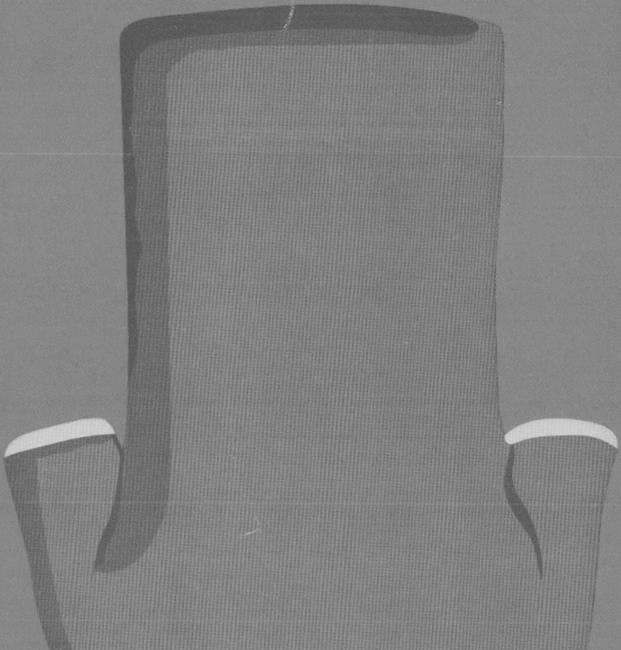

fish

poisson

(pwa-son)

aeroplane

avion

(av-ee-on)

spider

araignée

(a-ray-nyay)

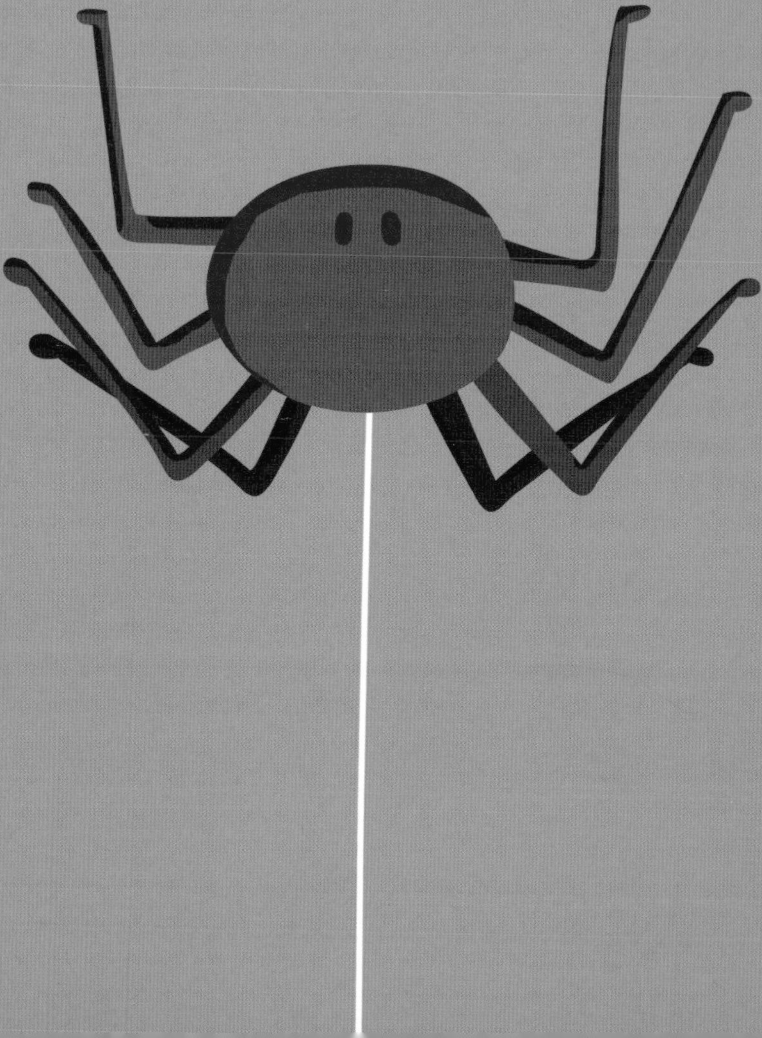

burger

---

hamburger

(om-buhr-guhr)

pen

stylo

(stee-loh)

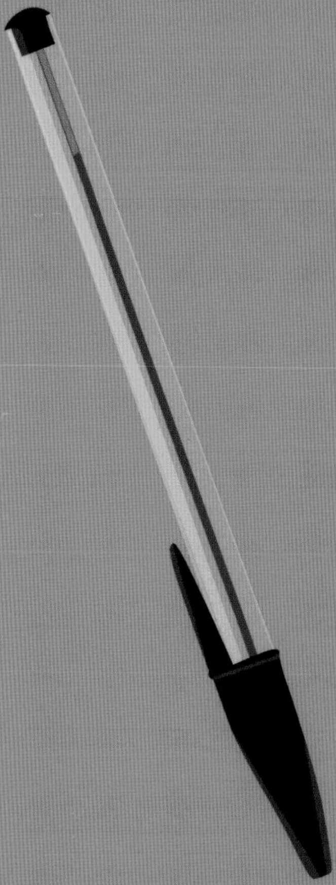

door

porte

(port)

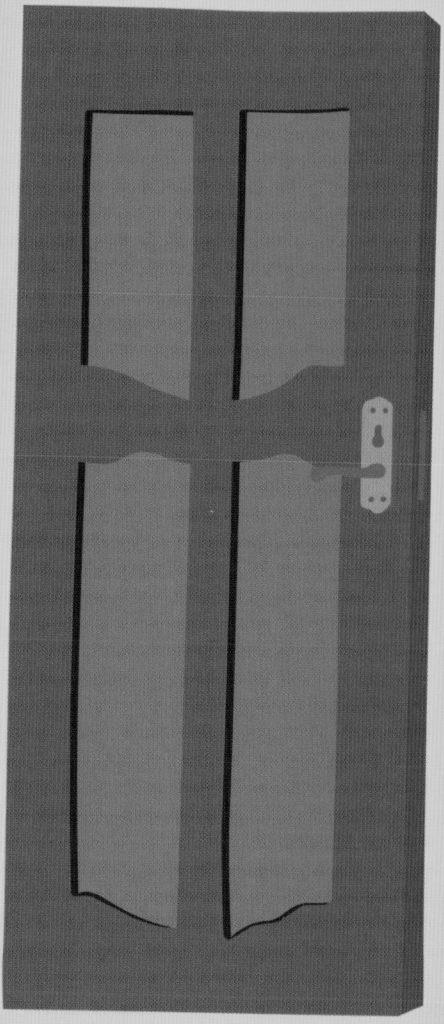

window

fenêtre

(fer-neh-truh)

curtain

rideau

(ree-doh)

tent

---

tente

(ton-t)

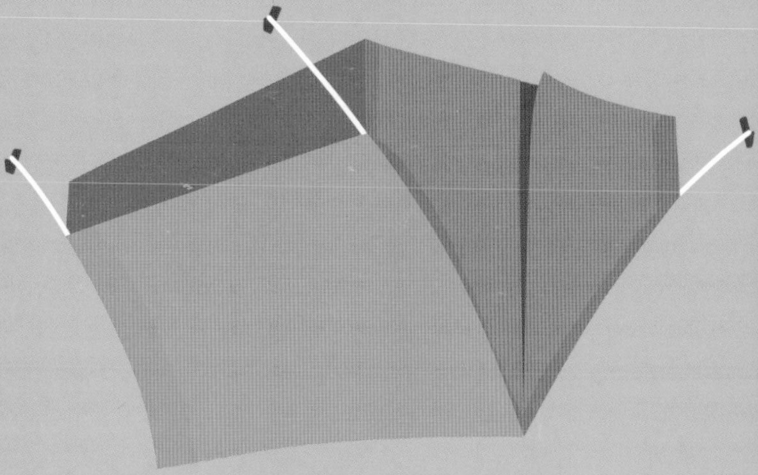

church

église

(eh-gleez)

tomato

---

tomate

(toh-mat)

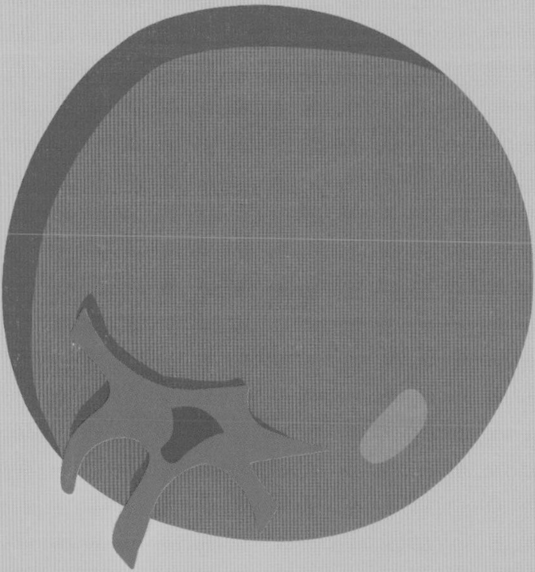

moon

lune

(loon)

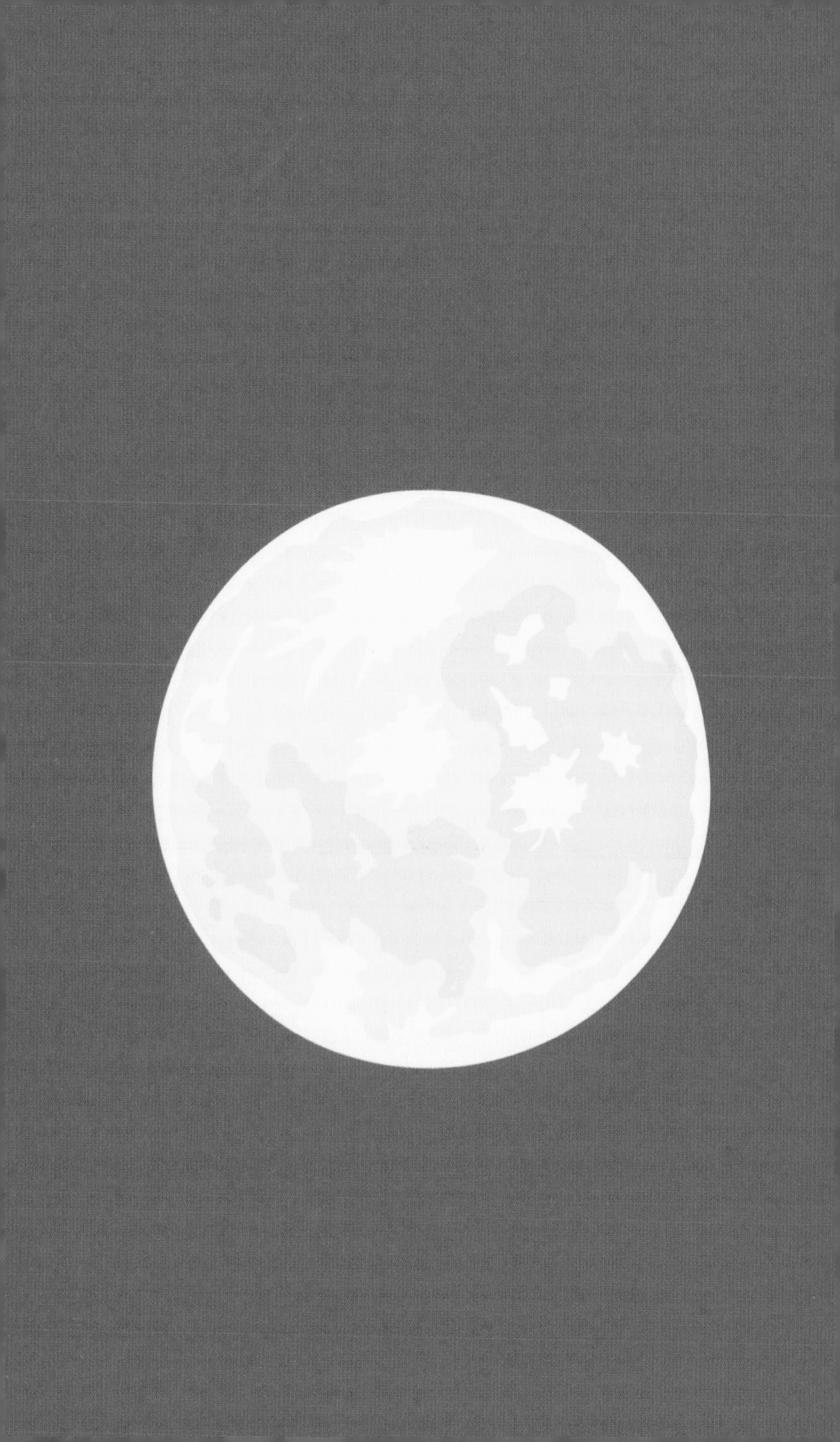

stars

étoiles

(eh-twahl)

postcard

---

carte postale

(kart poh-stahl)

stamp

timbre

(tam-bruh)

boat

---

bateau

(ba-toh)

goodbye

au revoir

(oh ruh-vwar)

au revoir